COO-EE
Call to Forest Recovery

by Lorraine de Kleuver

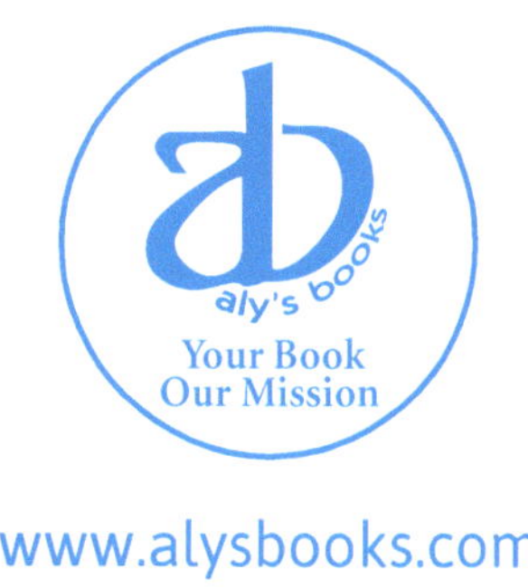

www.alysbooks.com

To William Kit.

This book is also dedicated to all forest recovery workers,
both professional and volunteers.

'Special Thanks' is given to Bruce Macpherson, ecologist and educator,
and Fiona Pfeil, educator and forester, for the generous time given
and invaluable suggestions in the development of this story.

We would like to premise this story by acknowledging the Traditional Custodians
of the Australian bushland and pay our respects to their Elders past and present,
of which this call is a part of their ancestral heritage.

The Adventures of Felix and Pip – COO-EE Call to Forest Recovery
Copyright © Lorraine de Kleuver
Illustration copyright © Lorraine de Kleuver

First Edition 2023
Published by Aly's Books

www.alysbooks.com
Your Book | Our Mission

ISBN: 978-0-6459030-1-0

After hearing their friends' wedding was postponed to the following weekend, Felix and Pip decided it was time to leave the wombat hospital. So, they said their goodbyes, especially to Wombatina, with whom they became great friends. Driving off, they talked of their memories at the hospital. That was until they heard a loud bang from the back of the truck.

"Oh my God," Felix cried out.

"Hang on!" cried Pip as she tried to steer the truck to the side of the road.

Soon, a big four-wheel-drive wagon drove up. The driver had seen Felix standing on the bonnet of the red truck, waving a yellow hanky. Pip was so happy that they stopped, she ran quickly over to them.

"Hello," she said, with her paws leaning against the wagon's door and tail wagging happily. "Are we glad to see you! Would you be able to help us?"

Pip hoped like heck that they would.

The two kangaroos came out and had a look at the red truck. One of them introduced herself as Kimberly and said her workmate was called Koen. While Koen walked over to the flat tyre, Kimberly said, "I have a friend in Bairnsdale that can fix it. He'll pick it up and call us when it's fixed. Is that okay?"

They both said, "Yes! That would be great."

"In the meantime, we're on our way to work. Would you like to join us?" Koen asked.

They both nodded in agreement.

"Okay, I'll call our workplace and let them know both of you will be with us."

Once Felix and Pip were safely placed in the wagon, they all drove deep into the forests of Buchan, where the hills were covered in burnt trees. Felix climbed up along the seatbelt so he could see out the window.

"Gosh," he said, shocked. "Look, Pip, lots of trees have fallen to the ground." Then, turning to Kimberly, he asked, "Kimberly, if all the trees are black, does that mean they are all dead?"

"No," Kimberly replied. "We will show you soon that many do survive with the help of a little magic."

4

Soon enough, they arrived at a spot where smoke haze was still around.

"This is our first stop where we clear roadways for forest equipment to come through," Keon explained to them. After placing a safety hat on Pip's head, he pointed out that, at all times, they need to wear protective gear.

"Why do we need protective gear when there are no fires?" Pip asked.

"See all those fallen branches, some are quite big and heavy. You wouldn't want one of them falling on your head," Koen warned.

"This is a great spot to have a break, and for you guys to learn a bit about forest recovery," Koen began to say.

Felix was the first to notice something moving. "Those little blue birds look to be eating tiny little bugs on those leaves," he said proudly.

"Well spotted," praised Kimberly. "Those little bugs like to feed on eucalyptus leaves, and, when they poo, they ooze out a sugary fluid that lots of small creatures and tiny birds like to eat."

"Hey guys, we have another job to do," said Koen.

"What will you be doing?" asked Felix, wondering what the job was.

"We'll be checking how safe some of the trees are. Letting other forest workers know which trees are unsafe," explained Kimberly.

"Hey, Pip," Felix called out. "Come over here. Look at this colourful butterfly."

Pip hurried over. "Wow, it's pretty," she said.

Then she saw a lizard coming down a tree towards it.

"If it's not careful, that lizard might have it for lunch."

Later, when Kimberly and Koen returned, they decided to take Felix and Pip for a walk. When they reached a different spot, Koen asked them, "Have a look around this tree, and tell us what you see here."

Pip picked up some yellow spongy stuff from the ground and asked, "What's this?"

"Well, I'm glad you noticed, Pip," praised Kimberly. "That is a type of fungi that helps the burnt soil to recover by protecting it from being blown away. There are all different types of fungi, and all of them have a special job to do. They provide food for insects and small and large animals so they can survive."

A bird flew overhead, squawking as it flew towards them.

"That poor bird has probably been flying around for hours looking for food," Koen said.

Koen walked around to see if he could find something for the poor bird to eat. He walked over to a casuarina tree, knowing that this bird likes to eat the seeds from inside the cones.

The bird leaned its little head on Koen's chest. "The poor thing is too weak to be afraid of us," he murmured. He gave the bird drops of water and helped it to eat a little more.

Once the bird looked like it had its strength back, it started trying to get away from Koen's protective hand. So, he lifted his arm up and let the bird free.

"Goodbye and good luck, birdie," they all said, watching it fly away from them.

While Kimberly and Koen had to do more checking of trees, Pip saw an animal moving amongst some ferns. When she went to walk closer, she saw something big and scary. Pip ran straight back to where Felix was.

"Hey, Felix," she called out. "There's a monster lizard over there, and it looks mean and dangerous," she said, breathlessly.

When Kimberly and Koen got back, Pip told them of what she saw.

Koen said, "It sounds like you saw a big goanna."

"Okay," said Kimberly, nervously. "I think we'll leave here and get away from it as quick as we can."

Once they were a long way from the goanna, they came across the most beautiful sight ever. There were yellow flowers everywhere.

"How beautiful is this!" Kimberly joyfully expressed.

"Wow!" Felix said. "It's like being surrounded by a sea of yellow; it's fantastic."

"How come all these flowers can take up so much space?" asked Pip.

"They have always been part of the forest, but because of the fires and having less tree cover, these flowers just take over and grow like crazy," Kimberly said, laughing.

"Amazing as these flowers are, they also help with forest recovery," Kimberly revealed. "The flowers provide nectar for insects and butterflies. Also, having such large numbers of flowers, all together like this, forms a massive umbrella, providing a hiding place for thousands of insects and small animals."

Koen suggested to Kimberly that they go and cool down at a waterfall nearby. "We can show Felix and Pip the little fish that are there."

Kimberly rolled out her backpack and called Pip over. "We will get there faster if I carry you in my backpack. Are you okay with that?"

"Wow, that would be great," answered Pip.

"Woo hoo," called out Pip, as she bounced up and down in Kimberly's backpack.

"I'm having so much fun," laughed Felix, held firmly inside Koen's pocket.

Both Kimberly and Koen just laughed. They, too, were having fun.

The four friends wasted no time in cooling themselves down when they reached the waterfall. Koen was keen to see how the tiny fish that lived there were doing. He hopped down the rocks to a small pool, taking a little net with him.

Kimberly called down to Koen. "I hope the water is better than when we last saw it."

"I hope so, too," he called back. "I'm really concerned about them."

"Hey guys, come and look at this little fish," Koen called out to them.

Holding it tenderly under the water's surface with both hands, he showed Pip and Felix the tiny galaxias fish.

"Aww," they both said. "It's so cute."

"Yes, it is. But I'm afraid to say that, after the bushfires, dirty, muddy soil flowed into this pool and killed most of the food that it eats. We may have to move them to cleaner waters."

16

Kimberly's mobile started to ring.

"Hello," she answered.

It was her friend, calling to say that the truck's flat tyre had been fixed.

"That's great," she said, and hung up.

Kimberley called out to Pip and Felix. "Good news, guys, your wheel is fixed."

"That's great," they both said.

"We best make a start and head back to camp," Koen urged.

When they returned to camp, they had snack time again. While having a rest, Felix explored a burnt tree. Curious about a bud poking out from the burnt bark, he asked Koen to come and look at it.

While eating his banana, Koen told Felix about it.

"That bud you're interested in takes some explaining," he said. "It's one of nature's most special recovery tricks."

After finishing his banana, Koen hopped over to where Felix was. Looking closely at the bud, he said, "This tiny bud is what I like to call The Bud of Hope."

While Koen kept talking, Kimberly carried Pip over so that they all could join in.

"When I look around and see thousands of burnt trees, I always ask myself, 'How can these tiny buds save those trees at all?' Speaking of which," I can see Kimberly's getting herself ready to to show you more about the epicormic buds."

Rubbing her paws into the black ground, Kimberly began drawing some dots and wiggly thin lines onto the log.

"See these dots," she pointed. "They are called epicormic buds. And these wiggly lines are called epicormic strands. It's hard to say, but if you break it up into 'epi-cor-mic', you'll soon be saying it right."

Kimberly explained, "When trees are burnt they can still be alive, providing they're not badly damaged. These tiny buds," she pointed, "are made to wake up. It's a bit like what you do when you wake up; you open your eyes, stretch your arms out, ready to get out of bed. Well, the tiny buds and strands do the same."

As Kimberly continued the epicormic bud story, she got Pip and Felix to imagine being an epicormic bud.

"Now, close your eyes and imagine that you're sleeping inside a tree. I want you to picture yourself as a pinkish tiny round thing about the size of a grain of rice. Okay?"

They both nodded.

"Now, all of a sudden, you've been woken up. Your tiny epicormic body feels ready to stretch out. You have this urge to wiggle about. Quickly, that feeling gets stronger each time you wiggle forward. Then you sense rays of light shining on you."

You now have poked your tiny head out from the burnt bark.

"Now, you are that little bud that Felix showed us," Kimberly continued. "I want you to open your eyes and stretch out your arms. We haven't finished yet. Remember, we're still an epicormic bud with a lot of growing to do."

"Okay," Kimberly giggled. "Little by little, you change. Now, imagine that your arms are growing more arms. Then try to picture in your mind all your fingers growing tiny pink leaves on them. This is nature's magic trick. You have now changed from a tiny bud to a growing part of your tree. As you grow stronger, your arms will become big branches, and more leaves will grow, but now they turn green."

"Wow!" they both said. "That is so amazing!"

Koen returned in time to hear Kimberly finish her epicormic story.

"It's quite a story, hey guys?" he asked in passing. "When I see those bright green leaves growing on those burnt trees, it cheers me up and gives me hope that the forest will recover."

While Pip and Felix got ready to go, a butterfly landed on Pip's nose.

"Hey, look at this," she called out. "Is this little butterfly a part of forest recovery?"

"Butterflies and insects are an important part of nature and forest life. In a couple of years, this forest will be full of life," said Koen. "But now we need to hurry so you guys can pick up your truck and head up to Gelantipy for the wedding tomorrow," urged Koen.

After returning from their friend's wedding, Felix and Pip were glad to be back home. When offering Felix some snacks, Pip wanted to talk about the experiences and friends that they made.

"We've learnt so much over that time," she reflected.

"What do you remember most?" asked Pip.

 Felix thought for a minute and said, "It was amazing to see hundreds of animals working together to save lots and lots of lives."

"Seeing firefighters from overseas, selflessly helping out our own, was awesome too," Pip added.

"From disaster to recovery – it's a big story, one we'll never forget," Felix sighed, thoughtfully.

"I agree; helping others always makes me feel good," yawned Pip, with eyes half closed.

Author's Notes

The Coo-ee Call

Years ago, long before mobile phones, indigenous people would use the Coo-ee call to let their family and friends know where they were. The Coo-ee call can be heard over long distances.

The call was so effective in being heard over long distances that it was used by many Australians, especially those who lived in the bush.

It may be an old-fashioned way of letting people know where you are. But just remember, when you lose your mobile and have no way of letting people know where you are, you can always give a loud call of 'Coo-ee'. The louder, the better, and the more you repeat the call, the easier it is for people to find you.

So have a go. Do what the big kangaroo did.

Cup your hands around your mouth.

Take a deep breath.

Don't call it out too quickly.

Call the 'Coo' part slow and long – coooooo

Then call the 'ee' part, with your voice sounding higher.

When you call Coo-ee together as one word, it should go as set out below:

COOOOOO – EE!

Loud and long, then quick and high.

Ask your Grandparents, I'm sure they will know. They might even be able to show you how to make music from a Eucalyptus leaf – just ask them.

Try practising it with your friends.

The Adventures of
Life Ring
Felix & Pip

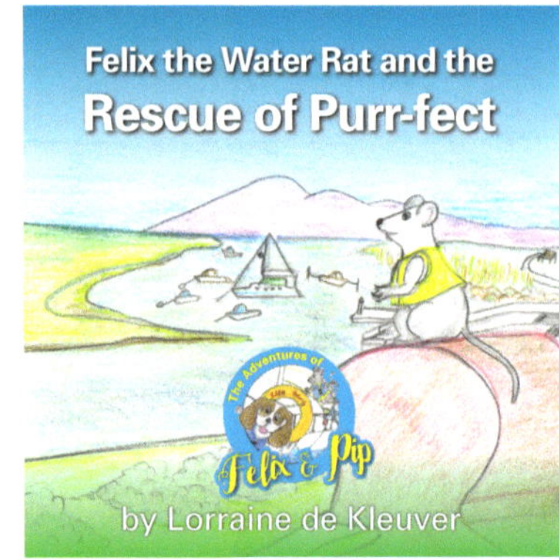

Felix the Water Rat and the
Rescue of Purr-fect
by Lorraine de Kleuver

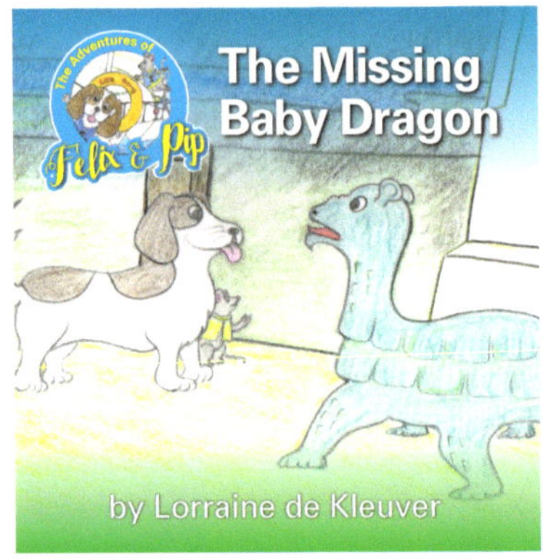

The Missing
Baby Dragon
by Lorraine de Kleuver

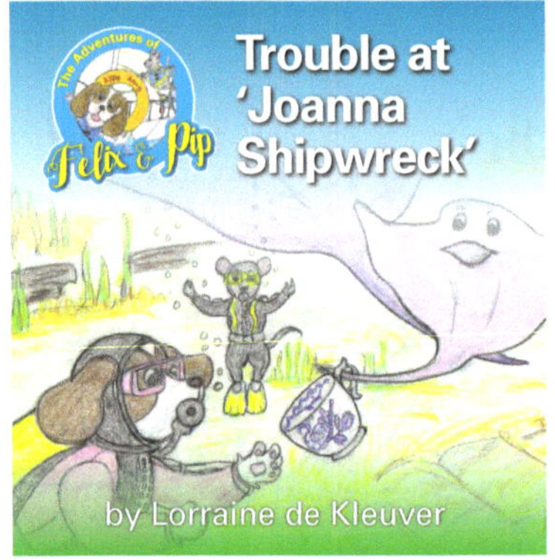

Trouble at
'Joanna
Shipwreck'
by Lorraine de Kleuver

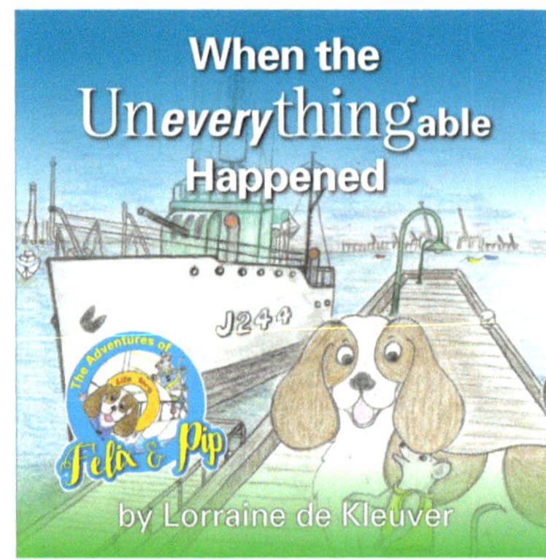

When the
Uneverythingable
Happened
by Lorraine de Kleuver

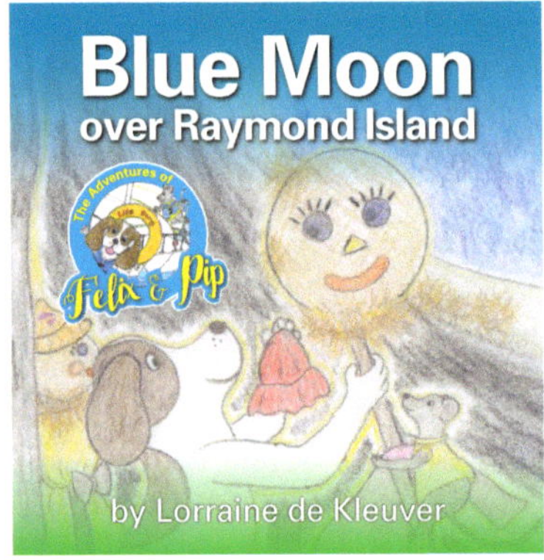

Blue Moon
over Raymond Island
by Lorraine de Kleuver

COO-EE
Call from the Bush
by Lorraine de Kleuver

COO-EE
Call to Friends Far Away
by Lorraine de Kleuver